BORN IN IRELAND MADE IN GERMANY

MEL KELLY

Special thanks go to:

Writing assistance: Ken MacBeth Knowles
Cartoonist: Henning Janssen
Cover and book design: Barbara Schelling

Born in Ireland
Made in Germany

ISBN-13: 978-1542453301
ISBN-10: 1542453305

Chapters

Introduction

James Joyce once wrote that to succeed as an Irishman you need 'silence, exile and cunning'.* Unfortunately, I'm not very cunning and I can't seem to stay silent; my only option was exile.

Many famous Irish writers have left Ireland: Joyce went to Trieste to write books and teach English whilst Oscar Wilde went to London to write plays and poetry. Following in their legendary footsteps, I went to Munich to write computer code and drink German beer.

But their exile was permanent. I was only going for six months ... or so I thought.

* The words of Stephen Dedalus, Joyce's literary alter ego, in *A Portrait of the Artist as a Young Man*.

Important Disclaimers

If you are looking for a politically correct text, do not read this book. However, do feel free to buy it.

If you do not like jokes about national stereotypes, do not read this book. However, do feel free to buy it.

If you are a sensitive soul, do not bother reading this book. But, of course, do feel free to buy it anyway.

Some early reviewers have warned that this book may permanently destroy my reputation. But since I don't have a reputation worth saving, it's a risk I'm more than willing to take.

If you've read all these warnings and you're still willing to read my story, let's get started quickly … before you change your mind.

Foreword

In the annals of etymology, a metamorphosis is defined as an organic change from one form to another. In nature, such a change is quite often from the ugly to the beautiful, like the caterpillar that changes into a wondrous butterfly. It is not so in Mel's book "Born in Ireland - Made in Germany". Here, the author Mel Kelly, struggles through his own metamorphosis, in which there is little visual change, but there is substantive change clearly visible at the bottom of a beer stein.

The book describes the wistful wanderings of a desperate full blooded Irishman seeking to find himself as he moves to Germany. All this is mischievously done in a mildly blue hue! Mel's move from Ireland is described in this book as a battle of culture, language and custom where nothing is sacred. He boldly goes where no man has gone before, albeit in a meandering sort of way.... and the only winner in this battle is the reader.

The book is riddled with anecdotes, stories of some disrepute and blurred observations in which are hidden some home truths about what it is to be Irish, German, and well, a blurred blend of both. Sometimes wicked, sometimes erudite and many times hilarious, the work strips naked the author both literally and figuratively as we are exposed to his journey – his metamorphosis.

Pick up a beer, even if it is an Australian one, put your legs up, settle down and enjoy "*Born in Ireland - Made in Germany*"!

Mark Hunter
World Champion of Public Speaking 2009
Gold Coast
Australia!

CHAPTER 1

Jobless in Dublin: Failed Table Dancer

It was becoming painfully clear to me that I had to leave Dublin. I was born in Dublin, I'd grown up there and I was happy there. Or at least happy in an Irish sort of way, which means my life was quite simple: I worked all week and drank all weekend. (The reason for the weekend drinking? To forget the week, of course.)

Ireland is the home of Guinness, the pub and big drinkers. *Alcohol Ireland* did a survey in 2015 and found that two-thirds of Irish people could be classified as alcoholics. I don't mind admitting I was shocked, truly aghast. I didn't know there were so many sober Irishmen.

But I was a proud Irishman. Whichever bar I went into, no matter how many other drinks were on offer, I always drank Guinness. I had a taste for the stuff, yes, but it was more than that. I stuck to Guinness out of my Irish pride, a sense of loyalty and an ingrained reluctance to try anything new.

Dublin is a magical place with a party atmosphere like no other; I was in my element there. Where else in the world can you order four beers one minute before the bar closes? It's not clear how you are supposed to drink them in this time frame, but that's part of the magic. And where else do people love alcohol so much that nobody can tell you exactly when the bars close? In other cities of the world there are set times for bars and clubs to shut. But in Dublin no one knows, except perhaps for the police. Even then, the information depends entirely on the mood of the particular officer you happen to be talking to – they might even join you for last orders.

When the bars finally do shut, thousands of people spill out into the streets in search of food. Not only is it a city of seemingly endless bars, Dublin also has a seemingly endless supply of quality fast-food joints. Though the word 'quality' should be taken lightly here: to be more precise, the food is of questionable quality; to be blunt, it's appalling. But magically, these same foodstuffs turn into Michelin-star fare with the addition of one simple ingredient: beer. After six pints of it, the previously inedible becomes inexplicably delicious.

Finally, the revellers take the magic bus home, wake up in the morning and have no idea how they got there. Dublin – my magical city. It's like a Harry Potter movie without the broomsticks, wizards and Hogwarts … and with a lot more alcohol.

In Dublin I also have great family and friends who are very supportive in an Irish sort of way. Being supportive in an Irish sort of way means that every time a friend or family member succeeds you feel conflicted. Whilst you're happy for them, there's a tinge of jealousy that leaves you with a sour taste in your mouth. That sour taste? It's very Irish, I assure you.

I wouldn't necessarily say that Ireland is a nation of *begrudgers*; no, I wouldn't say that. But people from other countries might. In America when they see the big house on the hill they say, 'Wow, one day, if I work hard enough, I can own a house like that.' In Ireland we say, 'Who do they think they are, having a house like that?' Or perhaps, 'They'd better be careful they don't have a fire. Water doesn't go up hills, you know.'

As Brendan Behan, one of Dublin's most famous and most

drunken sons, once said: 'It's not that the Irish are cynical. It's rather that they have a wonderful lack of respect for everything and everybody.'

Another reason I didn't want to leave Ireland was that I had a great job. I was working as a software engineer in the IT department of Guinness. (No, I'm not joking!) But really every job in Ireland is great. Where else in the world can you call in sick and the excuse of a hangover is more acceptable than a doctor's note? I just didn't realise how good I had it.

Not until disaster struck: I lost my job. The IT project I was working on came to an end and my dream job was gone. I don't want to make this more dramatic than it was, but I was devastated. It was 2003 and Ireland was booming at the time. It was the new Silicon Valley of Western Europe and I'd lost my job in IT. The irony didn't escape me, I assure you.

I searched and searched for a new job, but there were very few companies looking for the software skills I had. There was nothing out there for me and my imagination began to run wild. I found myself thinking, 'I don't want to end up earning my keep in a table-dancing bar.'

Eventually I had to conclude that no one would want me in a table-dancing bar anyway. I began to wonder if the fact I couldn't find a job was a sign; perhaps the universe was saying, 'Mel, it's time to leave Ireland.' But how could I leave Ireland, my Ireland? The land where the rain blows from the side and the only home I'd ever known. It was a dilemma. At the time I didn't think I could ever leave. Other people moved onto greener pastures, but there are no greener pastures than Ireland.

In the end, however, my hand was forced: the only job offers I received were in England and Germany, and I was broke.

England was an attractive option. If I went to the UK, the work would be interesting and the money would be good. I also had family and friends there. On the other hand, they'd left Ireland to get away from the Irish. They might not be too pleased to see me.

England, the home of the Premier League and the best footballers in the world, or I should say, the best-paid footballers in the world. England, which is at one end of the remarkable engineering feat that is the Channel Tunnel. The main problem with England, though, was that there were simply too many English people there. There was no getting round it. That was a part of the equation I just couldn't ignore.

And what about Germany? I had no family or friends there so I'd be starting with a clean slate. The more I considered this, the more it seemed like a real bonus, at least for the first few weeks. But then again I had the same problem with the locals in Germany as I did in England. Specifically, too many of them lived there. On the plus side, I couldn't speak a word of German: if they were all babbling away in a foreign language, perhaps it would be easier for me to ignore them?

So which was it to be? England: the land of beer bellies and football hooligans? Or Germany: the land of beer and the BMW? Because I'm a very mature and responsible adult, I made the biggest decision of my life in the most mature and responsible way possible: I flipped a coin.

I called it: heads for England; tails for Germany. The first toss landed heads. 'Okay,' I told myself, 'no need to make any hasty decisions. *Best of three*.' I threw again: it was tails. This was it: the decider.

The coin was sweaty in my palm. I tossed it up as high as I could. It seemed to take forever to descend and when it finally hit the floor it bounced violently and disappeared from view. When I found it underneath the sofa, I saw it was tails; the fates had chosen for me what I couldn't quite decide for myself.

Just to make sure I wasn't completely mad, I called my mother. In the background I heard my brother say, 'Just get a job, you bum.' My mum was a little more supportive: 'Both jobs sound good. Just pick one.' So that was it: I was moving to Germany. And little did I know what that country had in store for me.

CHAPTER 2

Goodbye Ireland; Hello Germany

The next few weeks went by very fast. It was a blur of packing, farewell drinks, more packing and even more farewell drinks – yes, things got very blurry indeed. But suddenly there I was, saying goodbye to my family and getting into a taxi with a modest selection of my worldly possessions.

Everyone at home thought I was mad – I mean, why would anyone in their right mind go to Munich or even Germany of all places? But I was starting to feel excited about my adventure. Yes, I was leaving my beloved Dublin behind, but it was only for six months … right?

In Ireland some conversation topics are taboo and one of them is religion. Though when I was growing up in Dublin the population was ninety-eight per cent Catholic, so it wasn't really much of a talking point. Ireland was so Catholic that Jesus himself would have been proud to be born there.

Today things are a little different. Whilst ninety per cent of the Irish population would still say they believe in God, only twenty per cent will publicly admit to being Catholic. (Actually I made this statistic up, but I'm pretty sure it's completely accurate.)

The Catholic Church went from a position of pretty much untouchable authority at the start of the nineties, to being considered worse than thieves, murderers and even bankers. They nearly managed to make Irish politicians look clean-living, honest and respectable.

Yet when I left for Germany, my family still worried about me. We were a typical Irish Catholic family and they wanted me to marry someone with the same beliefs as theirs. But I wasn't getting fooled into that. Why would I marry someone who also believes I'm an idiot? However, we did a little research and discovered that Munich began as a settlement founded by Benedictine monks some time around the eighth century; better still, the city's name originally referred to the *Munichen*, the pious Catholic monks who lived there. So my mother felt a wee bit more reassured as I waved goodbye to her from my taxi.

Bavaria is the largest state in Germany, in the south-eastern corner of the country. Munich is Bavaria's capital, home to over 1.5 million people and the nation's third-largest city. Yet despite setting off equipped with these facts, it turns out that when you arrive in Munich, you're never quite sure where you've landed.

If you look on the map, Munich is the Bavarian capital and Bavaria is most certainly in Germany. Sounds obvious, doesn't it? But as any Munich resident will be quick to tell you, Bavaria is not the same as Germany. And I found this out pretty fast.

As I walked through the arrivals terminal at Munich Airport, I saw a huge German flag hanging on the wall. On the flag was a massive eagle, which is the German national symbol, and the text: 'Welcome to the BRD'. For non-German readers, BRD stands for *Bundesrepublik Deutschland.* I had no clue what this meant at the time, so I asked a nearby policeman. He answered dryly, without missing a beat, 'Bavaria and the Rest of *Deutschland*.'

Ah okay, this was a joke. Whoever said that the Germans don't have a sense of humour? This guy was hilarious. We Irish could learn about humour from the German police all day long.

So next I asked him, 'Okay, so where have I landed?' Just as quickly he responded, 'Bavaria – that's not far from Germany.'

I was only going to be in Germany for six months, but if all the Germans were as funny as this guy, I wasn't going to miss Ireland as much as I'd feared. But I hadn't got to passport control yet ...

IRE
3

CHAPTER 3

German Airport Police: Don't Call Me English!

When you move to a foreign country, you're supposed to deal with the frustrations of cultural difference on a daily basis. So far all was going well for me in Germany, but this was about to change. Whilst going through passport control, a policeman asked me gruffly, 'Why are you coming to Germany? Most English people seem to have a problem with Germans.'

Now if we Irish have a weak spot, it has to do with the E-word. When you call one of us English, we change instantly from a happy-go-lucky lover of life into a very unhappy gremlin. Whether the policeman had made a genuine mistake or it was a deliberate provocation, he had definitely ruffled my feathers.

'Well,' I answered, 'there are two reasons. First of all, I'm not from England, I'm from Ireland. And second of all, we don't have problems with anyone … except the English.'

This encounter surprised me as I had always thought of the Germans as being not only well travelled, but also educated and knowledgeable. Shouldn't they be aware of the wonderful, unique relationship between England and Ireland? Did they not realise that after 800 years of English oppression, all Irish people carry a special place in their hearts for everything English? We Irish are not bitter. It's not as if we're holding a massive grudge, but we do love it when the English lose at football – and this happens a lot.

I'm not sure how familiar you are with Irish history, but I'll give you a very brief overview. A long, long time ago the English came to Ireland, and then? For a long, long time they stayed. And then they stayed some more. Yet there was a happy ending … they left … and went home … mostly. Oh, if only the Romans had come to Ireland, we might have straight roads and plumbing that works. To summarise: we didn't like the English back then and things have changed a lot since those days ... but we still don't like them. Or perhaps it would be better to say 'It's complicated', like a bad Facebook relationship status update.

Then in 2008, along with most of the world, Ireland was struck by a severe financial crisis. As you can imagine, we needed some money. Actually, we needed a lot of money. More importantly, being Irish, we needed money to buy beer. The first country to give us money was England. Well, they didn't exactly give us the money. To be clear, it wasn't a gift. By definition it was a loan and, as was obvious to everyone observing the transaction, it wasn't exactly on the best terms. They were lending at rates that would embarrass a Russian gangster. But they are English, after all. It's not as if you can expect too much.

Then in 2011 the Queen of England came to Ireland. It was her *first ever visit*. In fact, it was the first time a king or queen of England had visited Ireland since 1911. Some Irish people were very excited about it, whilst others didn't want her to come at all. Most of us didn't care one way or the other, except that her visit caused traffic jams, endless news stories about English royalty and it cost a lot of money.

The green dress she wore in honour of the national colour of Ireland was the week's biggest news story. I'm certainly not the most fashion-conscious person – I can hardly remember what I wore yesterday – but all these years later I can still remember the press going on and on about the green dress and that perfectly matching hat.

She came and then she went. Thankfully she wasn't blown up or shot. This might sound like an exaggeration, but given the history, some people couldn't be trusted with a box of matches during her visit. Thankfully nobody mooned her either. Who wants to see a naked Irish bum? Our exports may be highly sought after across the globe, but Irish Chippendales have never been much in demand.

One last thing whilst I'm on the topic: in June 2016 Britain voted for Brexit, to leave the European Union. Being from Ireland I have to admit that I was impressed. Take a moment to consider this and I think you'll see what an incredible achievement it is: it took Ireland 800 years to get rid of the British, while Europe managed to do it in only forty or so. We Irish have so much to learn about efficiency from the Germans and the French.

The most commonly spoken language in the EU is English. But after Britain leaves the only country with native English speakers is going to be Ireland. (Apologies to my Maltese friends, but with a population of only 450,000 people, you can't really be taken seriously as a country.) It got me thinking: the EU should consider moving all its institutions to Ireland. And the new official language of the EU should be Irish English. Why not? It is now the last bastion of authentic English in the union.

But that's enough about the English.

When I first arrived in Munich, I was impressed, very impressed. Munich was both safe and clean. The most important thing to me though? That's easy: some of the bars were open all night.

Additionally, right in the middle of Munich is a huge city park called the *Englischer Garten* or 'English Garden'. It's a funny name for a park right in the middle of a German city. Can you imagine Trafalgar Square being called Germany Square or Buckingham Palace being named Germany Palace?

In the English Garden, many Germans practise FKK with great enthusiasm. FKK stands for *Freikörperkultur* or 'free body culture'; it basically means walking, lying and sitting around naked in public places. A lot of Germans love taking their kit off in public at every available opportunity. This also happens in Ireland, but normally on a Friday night and only after ten pints of Guinness and a bag of chips.

Naturally, I was incredibly excited to check out FKK. On my first Saturday in Munich, I arrived at the English Garden early in the morning and eagerly awaited my first sightings. I was hoping for the German version of Baywatch meets Playboy. As the first people arrived and started undressing, however, I realised with dismay that it was going to be more like *The Full Monty* at a retirement home.

Nearly all the attendees were about as old as the Queen of England. You see, I hadn't gleaned one very important detail about FFK: it's much more popular amongst the older male generations than the younger female ones. Another learning curve and not the type of curve I was looking for.

CHAPTER

4

First Days in Germany: Doner, Dirndl and Dunkin' Donuts

As I was only going to be in Germany for six months, I wanted to try and embrace all things German. Okay, that might be a bit strong. But at the very least, I was interested in giving Germany a chance. As the saying goes: 'When in Rome, do as the Romans do.' But despite all the Italian restaurants here, and many Germans insistently telling me that Munich is really the northernmost city of Italy, it most certainly wasn't Rome. This was the capital of Bavaria, after all. This was Munich. Instead my motto would be: 'When in Munich, do as the *Münchners* do.'

So I watched closely and began copying what the locals did. I started to drink German beer every day, I ate German sausages and I wore my lederhosen – a pair of traditional German leather trousers.

A man wearing leather trousers might be viewed with great suspicion in other countries. He might even live in varying degrees of uncertainty about his personal safety. But if you want to be cool in Munich, you have to wear leather trousers. I may have taken it a little too far, though. As much fun as it is to wear lederhosen every day, I'm not sure you are meant to wake up still wearing them every morning. There's only one explanation for the fact that I regularly found myself waking up in these uncomfortable clothes: German beer.

Back in Ireland many years ago, there was a well-known public service campaign encouraging children to 'Just say no' to drugs, which, of course, is good advice for the younger generation and all generations. Considering the embarrassing situations I've got into whilst drinking beer, and especially those I've found myself in because of drinking *German* beer, I have now modified that old anti-drug slogan to: 'Just say no to German beer'. I have tried many times to say no to German beer, but German beer just doesn't listen.

But whilst my choice of drink was both an easy and a traditional one, my culinary experiences in Munich were initially, I'd be the first to admit, somewhat unadventurous. When I arrived, I frequented some of the finest restaurants in the city, places such as McDonald's, Burger King and Dunkin' Donuts. Why were these the best restaurants for me at that time? It was simple: I didn't need to speak German to order my food because they all had photos on the menus that I could point to.

You may not know this, but Germany actually has some of the finest food in the world. This includes *sauerkraut*, which is a particular way to prepare cabbage, as well as *kartoffelsalat*, a kind of potato salad that seems to be served with everything here. But one of the most German foods of all would have to be the *doner kebab*. Okay, this is a Turkish import, but it's become one of the most popular foods in Germany. And rest assured, they have plenty of pictures in doner restaurants too, so I was able to eat a lot of kebabs in my first few weeks in Munich.

Italian food is also very popular here. I've heard that the Italians worry about the quality of their food, whilst the Germans only worry about the quantity. And what about the English? Apparently they're concerned with neither quality nor quantity; they only worry about table manners.

We Irish aren't concerned about the quality or the quantity, and we definitely don't care about table manners. We are only worried that we eat enough to provide soakage for our trip to the pub later. For the non-Irish, 'soakage' means having enough food in your belly to absorb the alcohol you're going to drink that night. Isn't that the reason we eat meals anyway?

After I'd sorted the beer and the food, I had another problem: I needed to go to the toilet. However, the toilet doors don't have helpful pictures of a man or a woman on them. Instead they have the German letters 'H' for man and 'D' for woman, which confused me to no end. I would wait until another person went into the gents or the ladies, then, using my masterful powers of deduction, I would figure out which was the correct toilet for me to go into. Sherlock Holmes would have been proud.

The only problem with this little trick I'd devised? When nobody was around, I had to wait. On more than one occasion I found myself having to decide which was more serious: the call of nature, or the risk of going into the wrong toilet and looking like an idiot. If only I'd read the travel guides my mother bought me before I left, I wouldn't have had such problems.

There is a similar issue in Ireland where the letters 'M' an 'F' are used on toilet doors. It should be very simple, or so you would think: 'M' for male and 'F' for female. But actually, it's the other way round. The letters are for the Gaelic words: 'M' is *Mna* (Woman) and 'F' is *Fir* (Men). How I used to enjoy watching the tourists in Ireland trying to deal with this and no doubt my own toilet-based confusion was some kind of karmic revenge for all the fun I'd had at their expense.

There's another curiosity when it comes to German men and toilets. In Ireland when we go for a pee in the morning time, we stand at the toilet and hopefully our aim is good enough that we get most of it inside the bowl. If not, it's not so bad. We Irish men treat the whole bathroom as our toilet.

I used to think that this was a worldwide male tradition, but apparently it's not the case in Germany. Klaus, one of my new German friends, told me that he and most German men sit when they go for a pee. His mother taught him to do this from an early age for reasons of hygiene. Sounds logical, I know, but from an Irish point of view this approach just doesn't seem very manly.

They say that travel broadens the mind. But whoever said it obviously never lived abroad. In my first days in Munich, I felt like my brain was struggling with an information overload. And I hadn't even started my new job.

CHAPTER

5

First Job in Germany: No More Naps

At the beginning of my stay, my German skills were quite limited. Okay, non-existent. As I mentioned before, I couldn't even understand the letters on toilet doors. The Germans, as if it's not already enough to be good at cars and beer, are also very good at English. That's why I assumed communication wouldn't be a problem. Boy, was I wrong.

I thought my English was pretty good. But I suppose speaking English is like sex: everyone thinks they do it well.

In the first days of my new job I spoke what I considered proper English to my new colleagues. But all I got in return was blank stares and confused gestures. For some reason, despite my best efforts, nobody understood my flawless English. And I spoke the most perfect English you are ever likely to encounter ... I spoke Irish English.

They saw it differently though. They said I sounded like I was singing along to *Riverdance*. On top of that, I sounded like I was drunk. But I was stone-cold sober, I can assure you. I realised I had to speak much more slowly, more clearly and even to enunciate my words properly. And do all of those things at the same time. Unbelievably, my English improved … in Germany of all places!

This only created one small problem. The next weekend I called my brother for a chat. After we'd spoken for a little while, there was a long silence from his end of the phone. Believe me, this was very unlike him. I was just about to ask what on earth the matter was, but he got in first: 'Why are you speaking like that? Did you have a stroke?'

Another big difference between working in Germany and Ireland is punctuality. *Pünktlichkeit.* Just the sound of that word might shame you into being on time. *Pünktlichkeit.* Bloody hell. We Irish see an obsession with punctuality as a mental defect.

In the first week of my new job, the boss said to me, 'Mel, I need to talk to you about something. Could I have a word?'

'Of course.'

'Do you know what time we start in the morning?'

I had to think for a moment, 'No, actually I've no idea. I've never been here that early.'

Later in the week he said to me: 'Mel you've been late five days this week. Do you know what that means?'

'Yes, I know exactly what it means … it's Friday.'

I felt like telling my boss this instead: for us Irish, punctuality is more like sex. Performance is related to how late you come. But I didn't say that. It might be hard to believe, but for once I kept my mouth shut.

It's not just in the workplace, however. Everywhere in Germany punctuality is important. During my second week at work, I was at the station waiting for the train. The train was a little late and I noticed people were getting angry and frustrated. All these angry Germans around me stomping up and down the platform. They were on their phones saying things like, 'Sorry, but I'm going to be late. Really late.'

Okay, I know the train was late, but to be honest, the train was only two minutes late. I'm not exaggerating. Only two minutes. I can assure you this sort of thing would never happen in Ireland. Never. We don't even have any trains. Well, not many. We mostly have buses and they're normally very late.

So the train arrived, a little late, and it was time to climb aboard. Then something else strange happened: I witnessed first-hand how German people actually get onto trains. There was a massive swarm of people waiting, and, without wishing to sound old-fashioned, I couldn't help but find the way they pushed each other whilst trying to board rather unbecoming.

The way we queue in Ireland is completely different. For example, here's what two Irish people would say to each other as the doors opened and they tried to get onto the bus at the same time. Let's call them Michael and Patrick. That's a bit of a cliché, you might say. However, eighty-one per cent of all Irish people who are living and who have ever lived are called either Michael or Patrick. (I also made this statistic up, but again, I'm pretty sure it's completely accurate.)

Now as Michael and Patrick rushed towards the bus door, Michael would stop and say, 'You go first.'

Patrick would immediately come to a halt and respond, 'No, you go first.'

Then Michael would repeat with all his powers of persuasion, 'No, you go first. I absolutely insist.'

In moments like this I think it's no wonder we never get anything done in Ireland.

In fairness, the Irish are not the most efficient of people, apart from in the pub. That's where we could give the whole world a masterclass. Maybe that's why there are Irish pubs all over the world. And perhaps it's something we shouldn't be proud of … but we are.

But in Germany it's very different. Here you can see German efficiency in action. When you queue here, you lead with the elbows: bang! Then you go in with the head: thump! 'There's a gap,' you can hear them thinking. 'Let's go for it.' And that's just the grannies.

On the streets and in public places in Germany, it's all about survival of the fittest. Or perhaps a better way to describe it is that whoever has the sharpest elbows is going to win. Here are all these very respectable folk, but as soon as they get on public transport, they have absolutely no problem with knocking strangers out of the way.

In Germany it seems like queuing in a civilised manner is reserved for only one place, and that's the office canteen. People don't want to make a bad impression in front of their colleagues and can at least pretend to have patience in this setting. Anywhere else, such as trains and buses, it is total chaos.

Once I get talking about the differences between the Germans and the Irish, more and more things come to mind. On the train I noticed another major difference: eye contact.

In Ireland we are rather nervous about eye contact; it can be dangerous, very dangerous. If someone looks at you longer than a second, they might want to fight you … or give you a kiss … or both.

I hate to admit it, but in Ireland nobody ever looked at me, especially not any of the women. 'Poor Mel,' I can hear you saying, but it's the truth. Not a single look. As if I didn't even exist.

But what about when I was on the train in Germany? Well, in comparison to the Irish, the Germans are the world champions of staring. Now all the attractive German women were looking at me, which was great. But so were all the German men.

When I finally reached the office, after a super-efficient stare-filled commute, there was another big difference waiting for me during my lunch break. When we sit down in Ireland, there is noise, more noise and then some more deafening noise. We immediately start talking excitedly about the most important things in our lives, things of crucial importance … like the weather or football.

In other countries, talking about the weather is just polite small talk. But for us it's a survival tactic. We live on a wind-swept, rain-soaked island on the outer edges of Europe, so we have a lot of weather to talk about. Most countries have four seasons in a year, but in Ireland we can go through all four in a single hour.

Anyway, back to the lunch table in a German office. Let me set the scene: at first there is complete silence, more silence and then more deafening silence. The German lunch table is as quiet as a German football crowd after Ireland has beaten Germany yet again. The Germans sit back in stony silence and cross their arms giving lots of generous eye contact, just like on the train. With all this daily practice, no wonder they are the world champions of staring.

Eventually, after waiting what seems like an eternity, comes the first topic of conversation. With excitement they start talking about the most important things in German life, topics such as travel.

How many times have I been sitting at a table with Germans and the topic of conversation was how excellent their commute was because they made that impossible train connection? Everything ran according to plan and was punctual as it should be. Not quite Switzerland … but they're getting there.

Now that we'd exhausted the travel topic there was nothing more to discuss for the moment. So we went back to the same deafening silence as before. The Germans sit back once again in stony silence, cross their arms and engage in more overly generous eye contact.

There was something else about their behaviour that perplexed me. And only after many such lunches did I finally figure out what it was. Suddenly it all made sense … they were thinking about what they were going to say before they actually said it. This was a completely new concept for me: I often don't know what I'm thinking about until I hear it coming out of my mouth.

This was going to be a very long six-month project. But there was talk of a visit to the pub at the end of month. There was light at the end of the tunnel and hopefully it wouldn't be another oncoming train of cultural frustration.

CHAPTER 6

First Time in the Pub: Please Be Gentle

Finally, I was on familiar territory: we were going to an Irish pub. Obviously this wasn't my first time in an Irish pub in Munich, but it was the first time with my new German colleagues.

The Irish and the Germans both love beer, so I assumed this would be the perfect opportunity to get to know my new colleagues. However, yet again, I was in for a shock.

The invitation was for a Friday night after work, but with a curious start time of 21.00. And as my eyes scrolled down the email, I noticed there was also an end time of 23.00 – an end time? What nonsense was this? Was this a business meeting or were we going out for a few drinks?

So we were to meet in the pub at 9pm, or as the Germans say 21.00. (They like to be precise so that no one gets confused and shows up at nine in the morning.) We had agreed upon a plan and I fully intended to be punctual. You see punctuality is very important to me personally as an Irish person. That's why, with a lot of effort, I arrived at exactly 21.30.

My view of Germans up to that point had been that they were cool, calm and collected. Perhaps they are about some things, but certainly not when it comes to time. That I wasn't there exactly at the agreed-upon hour agitated them more than I could possibly have imagined. In that half an hour I must have received over a hundred messages: 'Where are you?' 'Are you lost?' 'Did you have an accident?' 'Should we call the police?' My goodness, it was clear to me now, there was no room in Germany for being fashionably late.

The group was a mixture of men and women, and the way they greeted each other was very Continental: hugs and kisses on the cheek and all that sort of weird foreign behaviour. Greetings in Ireland are a bit more distant, like far-side-of-the-room distant. It's what we're accustomed to and I wasn't sure I was ready for this new level of physical closeness.

That evening I learnt that in social situations the Germans

greet one another with a kiss on each cheek. Depending on the situation, the French can greet each other with up to three cheek kisses, whereas in Ireland that's about as far as some of us get on our wedding night.

So why had my new workmates invited me for this drink anyway? I'd assumed, just as we'd do back in Ireland, it was to make me feel comfortable and to welcome me into the team. I also secretly wondered if it was because they were so impressed by my sparkling Irish wit and wonderful Irish personality. However, not for the first time in my life, and definitely not the last, I was completely wrong. There was a much less-flattering explanation. They wanted to go to an Irish pub with a real Irish person; they wanted to get a taste of Ireland in the comfort of their home country.

Later I found out that they also thought it would be a good opportunity to practise their English with a native English speaker. Of course, unfortunately for them, they had not anticipated that they'd have such a hard time understanding me, especially as my particular style of Irish English speeds up dramatically after Guinness.

The more I thought about it, the more I wondered why anyone would want to take an English lesson on a Friday evening? Maybe the rumours about the German work ethic were true. However, I guess the setting was better than a normal language class. Here was a warm, inviting place with soft light and limitless Guinness on tap. What more could you ask for?

One of my new colleagues Fritz jokingly said that he'd heard an Irishman would never refuse a drink. Little did he know that this was no joke. In Ireland you never refuse a drink and I certainly wasn't going to start that sort of foolishness in Germany.

You may recall my surprise at the very efficient German approach to queuing, or to be more precise, not queuing. Unfortunately, this behaviour also spills over into the pub. That evening I first experienced what would become clearer to me over time: in Germany it is nearly impossible to stand in a pub with a pint of Guinness without being knocked into. In an Irish pub, Guinness is more sacred than holy water and spilling someone else's beer may result in eternal damnation. I don't think the Germans have figured this out yet.

Furthermore, when you go for a drink with friends in Ireland, it is unquestionably a social affair. When you buy a drink, you don't just buy a drink for yourself. You also buy a drink for everyone else in the group: this is known as a 'round'. When someone wants to have a second drink, the polite thing to do is for the next person to get up and buy a round for the whole group.

In Ireland this 'round' system is seemingly done out of a sense of generosity. At least to an outsider it might appear that the Irish are a very giving folk. One person buying a drink for everyone in your group is a clear sign of kindness, but there's more to it than meets the eye. This system saves you from going to the bar yourself every time you want a drink.

Still, the most important thing to remember is not to miss your go to get the round in. The people in Ireland may seem rather informal, but not standing up and buying a round of drinks when it's your turn would be an unforgivable sin and result in immediate social isolation.

But in the Irish pub in Munich I learnt the hard way that this custom of buying rounds hadn't made it to Germany yet.

If you buy a round of drinks for a group of Germans and are somehow expecting to get a drink back, you will be waiting a long time ... and waiting … and waiting.

You'll probably still be waiting when the polar ice caps finally melt away. Buying a round is just not the done thing in Germany. Your generosity might very well be appreciated, but there is no point expecting the favour to be returned. It's not that the Germans are mean or tight-fisted – no, not at all. Nevertheless, in some ways they do make the Scots look like big spenders.

I had now bought the first round of drinks and the beers were sitting on the table in front of us. I could already imagine the delicious taste of Guinness crossing my lips and, before I had time to consider what I was doing, I started guzzling it down. Oh no. Big mistake.

In Germany you have to raise your glasses to each other first before you start to drink. I'd heard something about this. Okay, fine. That sounded easy enough, so I raised my glass, looked round the table quickly and started guzzling again. Oh no. Big mistake number two.

When you raise your glasses to each other, you also have to make eye contact with everyone. I'm not kidding here. This is taken very seriously; Germans just love eye contact! This means looking at each and every individual in the group. 'My goodness,' I thought to myself, 'what a waste of perfectly good drinking time.'

If you do not make proper eye contact before having a drink in Germany, it is considered bad luck, very bad luck. I asked what was meant by 'very bad luck' and the answer I got was that you would have bad sex for the next seven years. I still don't understand that one. As a man, I have no idea what is meant by bad sex. As a man, either there is sex or there is no sex. Or as one of my American friends always says, 'Sex is like pizza. When it's bad, it's still good.'

But there I was, enjoying the beer and conversation, feeling rather German, enjoying the party in a pub in the middle of Munich. In some ways this had turned out far better than I'd expected. Then at precisely 11.00 pm (or 23.00 German time) my new group of buddies started getting up to leave. Wait just a minute: I was only warming up. It looked like I was going to be left there drinking on my own. I knew the email said 'a drink', but surely they didn't seriously plan to have only one drink and go home for an early night?

So I said to Klaus, 'What's going on? Do you have another party to go to?'

He answered, 'No, no. I just have stuff to do tomorrow morning.'

Reluctantly, I accepted his excuse. Then I moved on to Johann and asked him the same question. He responded, 'No, but I have stuff to do on Sunday morning.'

This was getting suspicious. So I asked Fritz exactly the same thing. He said, 'No, I can't stay. I have to go to work on Monday.' Wow, Teutonic punctuality and discipline all in the one evening.

The entire 'one drink' concept was completely alien to me. In Ireland one drink means the one drink you have before you have the second one, and that's the one before the third and so on. It couldn't be true, but sure enough, gradually they all left.

So there I was, sitting all alone in front of my Guinness and doing my best not to lose heart here in this new country. I tried to look on the bright side: at least I didn't have to buy any more rounds.

St Augustine is supposed to have said, 'The world is a book, and those who do not travel read only one page.' In my case, I was reading too many new pages all at once, and I thought it might be better for me to go back to Dublin and the page I already knew by heart.

CHAPTER 7

Promised Land: Beers, Bellies and Breasts

But then something happened.

I'd been in Munich for almost six months and my work contract was coming to an end. During that time, I had learned to live with the frustrations and misunderstandings of cultural difference. I was even getting quite fond of my daily intake of extremely healthy German food such as sausage and sauerkraut, and don't get me started on the German beer! But now it was nearly time to go back home to Ireland. I had got the money: it was time to cut and run.

A week or so before I was due to leave, my colleagues invited me to the Oktoberfest. Living in Munich I had already heard a lot about it. I knew it was the biggest beer party in the world with over six million visitors and packed with the best beers Munich had to offer. I had to see it before going back to Dublin.

The festival takes place on the *Theresienwiese*, a large open space in the middle of the city where the fourteen famous beer tents can be found. These tents are devoted solely to the traditional pastime of drinking as much of the purest German beer as you can, normally whilst dressed in traditional German clothes: *lederhosen* for the guys and *dirndls* (traditional Bavarian dresses) for the women, or the other way around if you prefer. You walk inside one of these massive spaces and look across a sea of big beers, big bellies and big breasts.

Get your minds out of the gutter there. When I say breasts, I mean chicken breasts. It's the traditional meal of the Oktoberfest: half a roasted chicken and a massive litre of delicious Bavarian beer. Okay, you can let your mind go back into the gutter a little bit: many annual festivalgoers say their trip isn't complete unless they get their fill of beer and all sorts of breasts.

The tents were packed full of revellers and there was an incredible party atmosphere. Everyone was sitting on long benches around narrow wooden tables and looking down the line at my new German friends, laughing and wildly happy from the delicious hops, I felt like hugging them all. It was the beer talking, naturally. But suddenly the divide I'd felt since the moment I'd arrived – between the city and me, between my new friends and me – seemed to disappear.

Okay, a lot of things disappeared that night – mostly memories. Yes, things were a little vague in my mind the next morning, but one thing did remain clear: I knew that I wanted to stay. Germany had become my Promised Land; there would be no more going back to Ireland. I had found my true home with my new German brothers and sisters. Who but the Germans could create something as wonderful as the Oktoberfest?

From that night on, the cultural differences that had been frustrating me no longer seemed a problem. Now those differences seemed more like opportunities to understand Germany and become even more German than the Germans themselves. I was determined to stay no matter what.

CHAPTER

8

German Honesty: The Truth Doesn't Always Set You Free

Now that I had decided to stay, I resolved to understand the Germans better. And one of the first things I needed to get used to was German honesty. The Germans have an international reputation for being direct and honest. There is a reason for this: because it's true.

One Monday morning at work, I was feeling sorry for myself, so I decided to look for a bit of support from one of my German colleagues. (Note to self: never do this again.) I said to Stefan, 'I feel old and tired. I've got lots of wrinkles on my face. Tell me something positive about myself that will help cheer me up.'

Stefan squinted at me over his desk and assessed me critically for some time before concluding, 'Your eyesight still seems to be good, doesn't it?'

I can only hope that Stefan adopts a slightly different approach when his wife asks him how she looks. I'm sure German women appreciate honesty at all times, but do they really want an honest answer when they ask, 'Does my bum look big in this?'

It's possible that they do, because in Germany even high-profile figures seem to insist on being honest at the most inopportune moments.

But there's a side effect to German honesty. Sometimes in life it is necessary to tell little white lies, and sometimes even big black ones. But since most Germans don't practise lying on a daily basis – unlike their punctuality and staring – when the need for a lie arises, they tend to get caught out and caught out badly.

Take Uli Hoeneß, a legend in Germany, winner of a World Cup medal in the 1970s, the president of Bayern Munich and to top it all off a multimillionaire. It would be fair to say that he walks on water. Well, at least on Munich water.

But in 2013 he got caught up in a tax scandal and couldn't lie his way out of it to save his life. His failure to pay nearly thirty million euros in taxes resulted in the most important transfer of his career ... to the local prison.

Then there's Franz Beckenbauer, another footballing legend from the 1970s and 80s. He was involved with FIFA for a number of years and it seems he was lured over to the dark side. When accused of bribery and corruption, he retorted, 'What's wrong with that? What else would you expect? This is FIFA.' (Full disclosure: I made this quote up, but it sounds true doesn't it?)

And of course the latest addition to this list of famous Germans who couldn't lie well enough is Volkswagen's former CEO Martin Winterkorn. During the Dieselgate scandal, he was forced to apologise for the fact that the company had intentionally installed software that allowed diesel VWs to pass emissions tests whilst actually polluting well above legal limits. Thus he managed to do two astounding things: he brought this world-famous company to the edge of bankruptcy and ruined the country's previously golden reputation, tarnishing the brand 'Made in Germany' forever.

If only he could have lied better, we would still be breathing in those toxic fumes in blissful ignorance. Ah, let's face it: the truth can sometimes be so problematic. My advice is, if you are German and are tempted to lie, don't bother. You don't practise enough to do it well. Just do what you do best and tell the truth.

Take Jürgen Klinsmann, one-time German super striker and former manager of the United States' national football team. I don't know how much you know about football, but in this game the USA are, for once, the little guys. To be perfectly honest, the Americans are lucky if they even qualify for a World Cup at all. So if they somehow manage to avoid losing in an embarrassing manner, everybody's happy. Or wait ... was that the Irish football team I was talking about? Being slightly rubbish is sadly a reality for both of these national teams. Anyway, you get the idea: the USA was not a favourite to win the World Cup in 2014. And you don't have to take my word for it.

At a press conference Klinsmann was asked if the USA had any chance of winning the competition. Most managers would try and put some kind of positive spin on their answer. In other words, they'd lie through their teeth. But being German,

Klinsmann gave a typically German answer: 'No, of course not,' he replied dryly.

It was a bit of a faux pas, especially as he was managing a team from a nation that believes it does absolutely everything better than everyone else. Well, when it comes to obesity, racial tensions and shooting rampages, I have to admit the Americans are in a class of their own. But we're talking about football here, and when it comes to this sport, they are mere mortals.

Having said all of that, it's still a mistake to say no to an American. It's about as clever as saying no to a kid in a candy store … or trying to take a gun away from an American.

And talking of America and honesty, that most noble of all arenas springs to mind: politics. America has just voted in a president who is very inclusive, tolerant and a role model for us all: Donald Trump. I think even Mother Theresa would be willing to give him her sainthood.

Donald, or 'The Donald' as he likes to refer to himself, has some very strong views and he's not afraid to share them. He is against gay marriage and believes strongly in 'traditional' marriage. So much so, that he has done it himself three times. The Donald is also anti-immigration. However, his first wife Ivana is a Czech immigrant and his current wife Melania is originally from Slovenia. Even Trump understands that America needs immigrants to do the jobs that Americans just won't.

He's not very positive about Mexicans either and wants to build a wall on the border between the two countries that Mexico will also pay for – apparently. And his logic is, as ever, impeccable: in short, the Chinese built a great wall once and look how many Mexicans they have over there.

The Donald also brought to the fore the most important topic in any presidential election race: sex. He was accused of being a small man because he has small hands; he said small men compensate by buying big cars. So what was Trump compensating for when he built Trump Tower?

It seems Trump can say and do what he wants, including boast about groping women, and still become the leader of the Western world. But his team must be praying he doesn't get involved in a sex scandal whilst in office like a certain other former president we all remember.

Americans may be the inventors of porn magazines like *Playboy* and *Hustler*, but in public they are very prudish when it comes to the subject, especially if it involves their president.

In fact, every nation seems to have a slightly different approach to its leaders' sex lives. In France if the president were accused of being involved in a sex scandal, they would probably shrug and answer in the typical French manner: 'Yes, and?'

If the scandal were in Italy, the Italian president would be offended and reply: 'What do you mean, only one affair?'

In Ireland things are very different. We see honesty a little like punctuality and an overattachment to the truth as something of a personality defect. We certainly don't like to let the truth get in the way of a good story. Besides, Irish politicians haven't been involved in too many sex scandals. Maybe it's due to the influence of the Catholic Church. Come to think of it, in the past few years the Catholic Church has had the monopoly on sex scandals.

Politicians in Germany don't normally lose their jobs over sex. However, if they have any minor indiscretion in terms of honesty they will be forced to resign. And these high standards can be found in the rest of German society too. Standard student practices such as plagiarising work or paying someone else to sit your exams for you are for some reason not acceptable in Germany. Whilst business practices that would be considered standard in many countries, such as bribery and blackmail, are again for some reason not okay here either.

A few years ago it was discovered that the then German President Christian Wulff had received some small gifts from some business friends, including an invitation to the Oktoberfest and a stay in a holiday villa. In other countries such gifts might be seen as the privileges that come with power, an entitlement or even a right, if you will. But in Germany this was seen as corruption of the highest order and led to the end of his political career.

I also appreciate German advertising for its honest streak. Take Ritter Sport, a chocolate brand that is something of an institution over here. Whilst not as well known as Belgium and France for its chocolate, Germany is pretty good at making the stuff. But why is it not so famous internationally? Perhaps it's to do with the marketing campaign. The Belgians and French sell their chocolate as sexy, sultry and seductive, whilst in Germany, Ritter is sold using the slogan: '*Quadratisch. Praktisch. Gut.*' A quick translation into English gives us their scintillating slogan: 'Square. Practical. Good.'

I realised I would have to work hard to reach the high standards of German honesty if I was to live here on a permanent basis. (Though I didn't see any harm in keeping a little bit of my Irish storytelling charm.) I decided to start by being honest about the appalling state of my German language skills.

CHAPTER 9

Learning German: Teutonic S&M

A vocabulary limited to food, beer and toilet-door signs was not exactly the basis for sparkling conversation and thought-provoking interactions with the locals. Now that I was staying, I really wanted to learn the native tongue. But German is far from an easy language to master.

I started trying to learn German by myself. Every day I struggled with it and every day I was reminded of a quote by the English classicist Richard Porson: 'Life is too short to learn German.'

Mark Twain also had a thing or two to say on the matter in his comic essay 'The Awful German Language', in which he notes, 'A person who has not studied German can form no idea of what a perplexing language it is.' He wrote this almost a hundred and fifty years ago and for my money his perspective is still as relevant as ever.

But despite these difficulties, I thought to myself, 'It's a language spoken by over ninety million people in Europe. Surely it can't be that difficult?' Boy, was I wrong. As I shed blood, sweat and tears in my efforts, I remembered that encouraging phrase, 'Where there is life, there is hope'. I doubled down on my study and gave it my best.

But the next time I spoke to my brother on the phone – he could understand me okay now – I told him about my new positive outlook. He listened patiently and then said matter-of-factly, 'Mel, in your case, there simply is no hope.' (Maybe the Irish and Germans do have the same outlook on honesty, at least sometimes.)

In the German language, there are also three genders: he, she and it. And every noun has a gender. This is very confusing for English speakers. For us, all objects, all nouns are neutral; inanimate objects are neither a he nor a she. I'll admit I'm baffled by the gender of objects in German. Why does an object have to have a gender to begin with?

Let me give you a few examples to make my point. A table is a he, as is the chair beside it. Meanwhile the nearby lamp is a she. Logical, isn't it? No, not at all. There's no rhyme or reason to any of it. What if you're thirsty? What gender does a glass have? Well, in German, a glass is officially an it. Sounds crazy, doesn't it? Well, yes it is.

I discussed with a German friend the gender of objects in his language and how crazy the whole thing is. The table. He's a table. Why is the table a he? Is this table somehow masculine? Does the table have a penis?

He told me, 'Yes, of course. The table has four.'

I'm not sure if you find this funny or not. I can assure you that I didn't. But my German friend couldn't stop laughing for two days. Not only is the language different but the German sense of humour is a bit different too.

Normally in Germany, they think of everything but there are certain things that even the Germans haven't considered. A few years ago, the Austrian winner of the Eurovision Song Contest was Conchita Wurst. In case you didn't know, *conchita*

is the Spanish slang for vagina and *wurst* is the German slang for penis. Technically, that would mean that Conchita Wurst is both a he and a she. So how do you handle that one in the German language?

All this does mean that when learning German grammar you constantly have to think of sex. Well, you have to think of the gender of the nouns. But this had enough to do with sex to keep my interest.

In Ireland not many people are interested in speaking a foreign language and even fewer can actually speak one. By comparison many Germans speak more than one language. In fact, it seems like most Germans can speak multiple languages fluently. And as a rule they are very enthusiastic about foreign languages. If they are going on holiday to Spain the next year, they will do a Spanish course every week for the year beforehand. From an Irish point of view such behaviour is unthinkable.

However, I wasn't likely to be going on any holidays for a while. I had to stay in Munich and learn German. Or at least try.

CHAPTER 10

German Punctuality: Who Comes First?

My attempts at learning German by myself were not working out very well, so I signed up for a class. The students were from all over the Europe, and the first word our teacher Hans taught us was 'punctuality'. Yes, *Pünktlichkeit* again.

I know I've mentioned this before, but believe me, punctuality is a recurring theme in every part of German life. You can try and avoid it, but you do so at your peril!

Being in a class full of other people struggling to learn German was certainly a lot more productive than struggling at home on my own. But it was still a hard slog. As I've previously alluded to, German is a very complicated language full of complex sentence structures, confusing rules about the gender of nouns and very long words. As Mark Twain reports in 'The Awful German Language': 'In the [German] hospital yesterday, a word of thirteen syllables was successfully removed from a patient.'

In order to make learning German slightly more fun, the class organised an outing. We were international representatives for our countries and we wanted to do something refined, cultivated … and cheap. Some bright spark suggested a city tour, but we all lived there; someone mentioned that Munich has some highly regarded art museums, but that was way too much culture for my liking; finally, someone suggested a visit to the world-famous Hofbräuhaus. Now we were talking my real language.

The Hofbräuhaus is a beer hall, rather like a mini-Oktoberfest. Whilst, tragically, Oktoberfest only lasts two weeks, the Hofbräuhaus is open all year round. For me, there was no other possibility and luckily everyone in the class agreed it was a good idea. After all, we needed to relax and have fun after our strenuous linguistic efforts.

I sat back, letting the good news sink in: I now had an excuse to go to the Hofbräuhaus, as if I really needed one, and I wouldn't have to wait months and months for the Oktoberfest experience. There was a god, or at least there was a beer god up there somewhere.

On the evening of the class outing I was a little late, ten minutes or so. For me, this was the equivalent of being half-an-hour early – I was getting better. But when I arrived at the bustling beer hall, my German teacher Hans was already there. He was sitting all alone and he was clearly annoyed. Although I was fairly proud that out of all the various nationalities represented by my class, it was me, the Irishman, who'd arrived first, Hans didn't see it like that. By German standards I was outrageously late.

So I thought I'd try and cheer him up. I didn't know much about the guy, but I knew he was a German teacher. So surely he'd love German grammar? Right? It was a foolproof plan.

Being honest, I also wanted to see if he knew the well-known joke about another very important German word: *arschloch*. For all you non-German speakers out there, it's the German word for 'asshole'. And even Mozart got involved in the low-brow humour of this word: he wrote a canon for six voices in German entitled, *Leck mich im Arsch*, which roughly translates as 'Kiss my ass'. And when modern-day Germans are annoyed with you they might say '*Leck mich am Arsch*', which funnily enough means the same thing.

So I turned to my German teacher, who was still visibly annoyed at me for being late, and asked him about the gender of *arschloch*: 'Which is the correct article? Is it *der*, *die* or *das*?' (That is, is it a *he*, *she* or *it*?)

Without missing a beat, a smile spreading across his normally sour-looking face, he said, 'No, Mel. It's none of those. It's *du arschloch*.' Which translates as, 'You asshole.'

Whoever thought that learning German could be so much fun? Beer and swear words were certainly keeping my interest in this complex language alive.

CHAPTER 11

Conversations in German: Girls, Gays and God

Once I started taking German lessons, I never stopped. I'm an enthusiastic if rather slow learner and need all the support I can get. One thing that immediately became clear to me, however, was why many others in the class, from a wide variety of European countries, were also keen to improve their language skills.

Our tutor was determined to teach us German grammar, but we had our own motives for learning. We were focused on much more important things such as meeting German girls. We were all searching for a single phrase that would instantly enhance our dating chances in Germany, and each of us had already decided what that crucial sentence would be.

The French guy wanted to learn how to say, 'You are so beautiful.' Typical Frenchman. There he was trying to uphold the French people's international reputation for being the best lovers in the world.

The Spanish guy wanted to learn, 'Your sister is so beautiful.' This type of approach might work in Spain, but it's not guaranteed to work anywhere else. Frankly, I'd be surprised to hear that it worked all that well in Spain, but I suppose I should give him the benefit of the doubt on this one.

Finally, it was my Italian classmate's turn. He wanted to know how to say, 'Your mother is so beautiful.' For the Italian man, the mother was, is and always will be the most important woman in his life. Apparently even if the mother in question is not his own.

To my mind, these civilised and romantic Europeans were just beating about the bush. I wanted to learn a far more important phrase. The first thing I figured out how to say in German class was, 'One beer for me and one beer for her.'

Ireland has a talkative culture, some might say too talkative. However, put me in a German lesson where I actually have to speak in German and what's the result? Complete silence.

Hans, our trusty teacher, would try to trick me into starting to talk. Even if I was speaking German very badly, he told me, it was better than not speaking German at all. He even went so far as to ask lots of questions about Ireland. I don't think he was just pretending to be interested, as obviously everyone in the world is fascinated by Ireland. Aren't they? Please tell me it's true.

Hans asked me to tell him what Ireland's three greatest contributions to the rest of the world were. I answered that we'd given the world its finest drink, Guinness, the finest places for entertainment, Irish pubs, and indeed some of the finest music in the world – of course, I'm talking about the Kelly Family.

Given that I was speaking German, I'm not sure if this was the best sales pitch for Ireland, but I had given it my best and covered some of the most important areas.

In 2015, when I was still taking German lessons, there was a qualifying match for the Euro Championships in which Ireland beat the Germans for the first time ever in a competitive game. It was one of the best moments in our recent footballing history and the home crowd went absolutely wild.

I explained to Hans that, to my surprise, my German work colleagues couldn't seem to handle the result. I got the silent treatment for a month. It was just like lunchtime, but all the time. Whilst Hans was impressed with my improved language skills, he didn't seem to think there was anything strange about my work mates' behaviour. He explained to me, 'Mel, the Germans are not as accustomed to losing as the Irish.' I couldn't argue with that.

That same year, I also found myself explaining to Hans that 2015 was a big year for Ireland for another reason: same-sex marriage was made legal. And we were the first country in the world where the people voted for the law to change.

To be clear: the Catholic Church was completely against this – very much so – and many Church leaders advised their flock to vote against it. Now that it has been voted through successfully and gay people can marry, the priests insist that God will destroy Ireland. But even if the priests are right, the gay community will be sure to do the most beautiful renovation job.

But the thing that really confused me about the whole thing, as I tried to explain to Hans in my faltering German, was why gay people were so excited about being able to get married. Had they not learnt anything from observing couples in the straight community? Now that the laws have changed, the gay community can be as unhappy as straight people have been all these years.

Germany was really having a positive effect on me. When I first arrived, my conversations consisted only of requests for beer and bad chat-up lines. Now I had picked up an interest in current affairs and could even discuss them in a foreign language. Not so bad for just over a decade in this wonderful city.

CHAPTER

12

German Engineering: Is Bigger Better?

As I mentioned earlier, I'm a software engineer, an Irish software engineer. And Ireland is the home of the most spectacular and successful engineering feat of the twentieth century … the Titanic.

My German colleague Fritz told me, 'To be a German software engineer means to be reliable, punctual … and alcoholic.'

Unsurprisingly, this conversation sparked my imagination and I began to toy with the idea of becoming a German software engineer. The more I considered it, the more excited I became.

Germany, the land of great cars: the brilliant BMW and the magnificent Mercedes. And let's not forget the incredibly reliable and sexy Trabant. Yes, the German car industry with the highest standards of engineering precision and the highest standards of honesty, integrity, and compliance. Just ask my friends over at Volkswagen.

Germany, the land of engineering feats: in the seventies they built the Olympic Stadium here in Munich; in the noughties the astounding Allianz Arena was constructed; and at some point in the distant future, the long-awaited Berlin Airport will open. For the non-German readers amongst you, Berlin Airport was due to be opened in 2010; at the current rate of progress, it will probably open in 2050.

Fritz told me something else about German engineering skills and it wasn't what I expected. There are many types of engineering that the Germans excel at and this includes medical engineering, or to be more precise, let's call it cosmetic engineering. There are many cosmetic operations out there for women and for men. But in Germany, most men seem to go for the same one … the extension … and it's not a hair extension.

I thought Fritz was joking, so I did some research on that most trustworthy of all resources, the Internet. But he wasn't kidding me: the worldwide home of penis enlargement operations is Germany. There are 15,000 operations of this nature globally every year, if you can imagine. And twenty per cent of those 15,000 are carried out in Germany. Maybe the Germans weren't as confident as they'd always seemed to me.

Later that day I was in the pub, like nearly every day to be honest, and here's what some of my German friends said on the subject:

First Stefan: 'We Germans don't need this operation. We have our Porsches and BMWs.'

Tobias continued: 'Okay, twenty per cent of these operations might be done in Germany. But I bet the other eighty per cent are done in Ireland.'

Then Chris chimed in, 'This is a point I could expand on.'

Laughing, Steffi and Anna added, 'It's great, isn't it?'

But I was still curious. Why so many penis enlargements? And of all countries why is Germany the place to get one? This is the best answer I could come up with: quite simply, it's the perfect storm. You've got German porn, German pragmatism and most importantly, you've got German engineering.

Any lingering doubts were further allayed the next time I was at the Oktoberfest. I saw a guy peeing on the side of a tent. In English the word 'gross' means 'disgusting', while the same word in German means 'big'. I proceeded to tell the guy peeing on the side of the tent, 'Uh, that's gross.'

The man turned to me, smiled broadly and responded to my statement by saying, '*Danke.*' He turned in my direction with his full glory on display, whereupon he exclaimed, 'I've just had the operation!'

I was trying my best to embrace all parts of German culture, but maybe there were some parts that were better left untouched?

STOP

CHAPTER 13

The German Accent: Permanently Drunk?

There is a stereotype about the Irish being drunk all the time, which was starting to seem a little unfair to me given the huge effort I was making to consistently turn up for work sober. But, even in Germany, you make one little mistake and those Irish stereotypes come back to haunt you.

I'd got into the habit of cycling to work. Munich, like many major European cities, is very cycle-friendly and the habit was helping me exercise off at least some of the beer I was consuming. But one day on my way to the office I unwittingly committed a crime, at least it's considered one in Germany: I rode my bike through a red light. I didn't realise how serious this was. And anyway, there was a police car right behind me that did exactly the same thing. So how bad could it be?

As it turned out, the police car going through that same red light was actually in hot pursuit of a runaway criminal – i.e. me. They pulled me over and to my astonishment demanded to see my driver's licence. But I was only on a bicycle. Luckily my German wasn't good enough to argue the point, so I handed over my driver's licence, my Irish driver's licence. Naturally, the policeman didn't recognise it.

The Irish driving licence used to consist of a piece of pink paper that looked like an ancient relic from medieval times, plus most of the information on it was in Gaelic. As for the place of issue it didn't say Dublin, but instead used the city's Gaelic name *Baile Atha Cliath*. This made such a licence obviously extremely useful and practical when travelling abroad.

Not surprisingly, the officer didn't understand Gaelic and proceeded to ask me where I was from. When I told him, his immediate comeback was, 'So you are drunk?' I nearly responded by asking him why he wasn't wearing his lederhosen, but I kept my mouth shut for only the second time in my life.

Then he asked me for my address. Now, I've documented the difficulties I've had learning the German language, but I haven't mentioned that the accent is also very difficult for us Irish to master, particularly when we're under stress. To make matters worse, my German address contained letters like 'z', 'ü' and 'ß', which aren't easy to pronounce: my street is called *Zweibrückenstraße*. This is not an address that I can say without sounding like I have a speech impediment. And here I was under pressure from the German police. So I made a mess of it. The officer laughed and said to his colleague, 'Definitely Irish and definitely drunk.'

This was discrimination of the highest order. I considered bringing the case to the European Court of Human Rights. I wasn't drunk … at least not as far as I could remember. But more than anything, I was frustrated. I was annoyed that I couldn't say my address properly in a German accent without sounding inebriated, so I decided to take action.

I went to a speech therapist to improve my pronunciation. When I told my Irish friends in Germany about it, though, they were perplexed: 'What's wrong with sounding Irish?' And when I told them that the Germans thought I sound permanently drunk, they were even more confused: 'And?' 'Well, aren't you?'

The German language is difficult. The words are hard and the grammar is tortuous. But trying to master the German accent? That's absolutely impossible. In case I got hauled over by any more policemen, my speech therapist and I immediately began work on pronouncing my German address, in which I discovered there are twenty-six German phonetic sounds. Unbelievable. Twenty-six? I thought the best thing I could do was simply move to the English Garden.

As an aside, there is a Welsh village with a name that contains fifty-eight letters, which makes it the longest place name in Europe. It's called: *Llanfair-pwllgwyngyll-gogery-chwyrn--drobwll-llan-tysilio-gogo-goch*. My Welsh friends in Munich can pronounce this village name with ease, but even they have the same problems when they try to say *Zweibrückenstraße*.

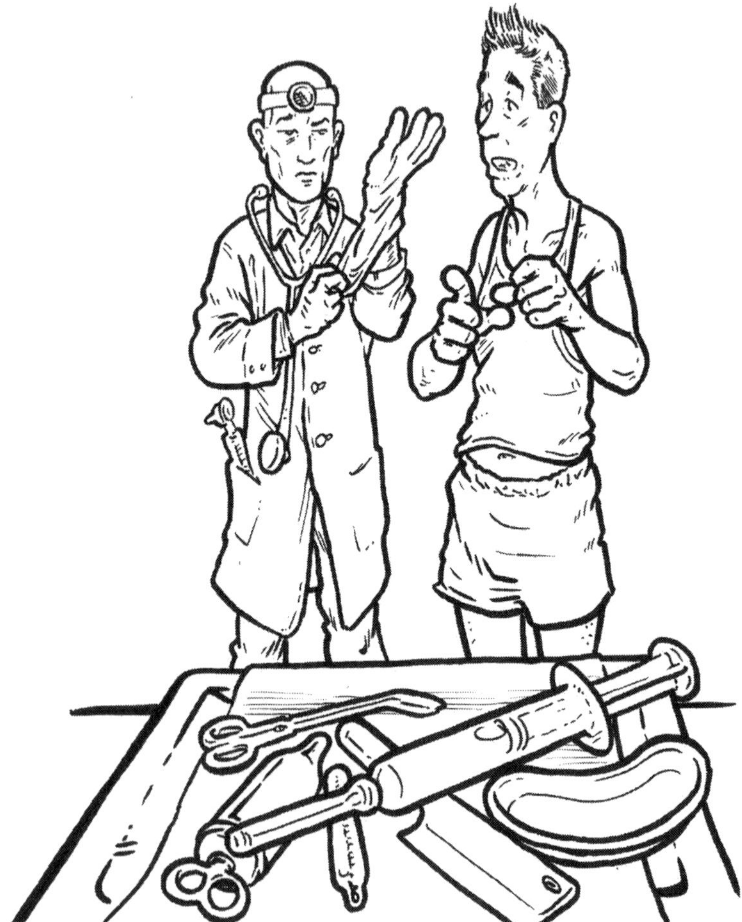

CHAPTER 14

German Health: Don't Get Left Behind

The longer I lived in Germany, the more I embraced German habits. One of these was the German fascination with all things medical. Another very noticeable difference between German and Irish people is the former's obsession with health. In Ireland there's a complete lack of interest in such matters, but one could argue that the Germans are prone to a little hypochondria. Most Germans I know have some form of medical complaint. To be clear, any German who doesn't have a medical complaint is either asleep or dead. By way of contrast, we have an old saying in Ireland: 'Most Irish only go to hospital twice in their lives: when they are born and when they die. Both visits are optional.'

Germans strongly believe in regular health check-ups, lots of health check-ups, health check-ups for everything. Eyesight check-ups, check-ups of one's feet and, of course, don't forget the check-ups for those perfectly white shiny teeth. Yellow and crooked teeth are nowhere to be seen in Germany, whereas in Ireland it's a badge of honour to have a mouth full of discoloured teeth.

There is one health check-up, however, that even the Germans aren't keen on. In fact, like the rest of the world, they're afraid of it. You see, we men spend much of our lives trying to convince people of how macho we are, but in reality we have many fears. Too many fears to provide you with an all-inclusive list, but the top three are as follows:

Number one on the list is talking to a pretty girl.

Number two involves managing to sustain a conversation that isn't totally nonsensical with said pretty girl. (This is difficult because you're so astonished she's giving you the time of day that there is a complete overload to your system that can result in a temporary paralysis of all bodily functions. This could mean slurring and drooling for no apparent reason.)

Finally, the third biggest fear is this particular health check-up; the one that could save you from an untimely demise. I'm referring, of course, to the prostate check, which for our purposes will be affectionately referred to as the bum check.

There is a rumour out there that if a guy pees on a pregnancy test and it comes back positive, he has prostate issues that should be checked out immediately. This test seems too good to be true. However, it is gaining traction in the world of medical expertise otherwise known as the Internet. But I was determined to do things properly like one of the locals; I wasn't going to skip the full physical check-up.

Why do men have such fear of this routine procedure? What's the big deal, after all? Let me tell you, the deal is big and our fears are real. First of all, the doctor may not be a real doctor. Secondly, the doctor may enjoy the procedure. And finally, and this might be the worst fear of all, in the midst of the doctor exploring my prostate, I might actually enjoy it too.

Reluctantly, I dragged myself to the clinic to get the dreaded bum check. At least there was one positive about being there: the nurses were beautiful. They were hot, even. The doctor, however, was not. It's going to sound like a caricature, but I swear it's true. This doctor, this proctologist, was a fat, bald, sweaty man with a dirty smile and big sausage fingers.

As the doctor led me into the examination room, he immediately said, 'Please take your clothes off, Mr Kelly.'

Being Irish, I am simply not that comfortable with being naked, so I nervously took off my T-shirt. The doctor looked at me impatiently, 'And your trousers.'

With the deepest of breaths, and with what I'm sure was a look of desperate determination, I nervously took off the rest of my clothes: my trousers, my underpants and even my socks. Now that I think about it, I'm not sure the removal of my socks was entirely necessary, but I panicked.

The doctor told me to go to the table and bend over. I bent over slightly, very slightly – an Irish kind of bend over, which I would say is done rather modestly. But he immediately barked at me, 'Bend over more!'

So I did as I was told. I bent over to a ninety-degree angle and braced myself for the worst possible intrusion that a heterosexual male can imagine. I could tell you what happened next, but I'll leave out the details and save those visuals being etched on your mind for the next month.

After what seemed like an eternity, the medical invasion was finally behind me, as it were. I pulled my trousers up with relief and asked the doctor if he'd found anything. But before he had a chance to reply, there was a knock on the door and he abruptly left. A nurse entered the examination room and frowned at me: 'Who was that man? The doctor took longer than expected with another patient, but he'll be with you any minute now.'

Okay, I'm kidding about that last part, but the rest is true. And I won't pretend I'm not tempted to try the pregnancy test next time.

Even so, this was a very different Mel Kelly to the one my friends knew back home in Dublin. What was happening to me? Was I starting to change? I was taking my health seriously, going for regular check-ups, no matter how unpleasant, and I was starting to exercise more, eat better and even drink less. But despite all this daily German bliss, trouble was looming on the horizon.

CHAPTER 15

German Passport: Showdown at High Noon

After more than a decade of living in my Promised Land, there was talk of Brexit. If the UK were to leave the European Union, what would Ireland do? The glue that keeps the EU together for the Germans, as well as most of the other countries in the EU, is the notion of peace in Europe. That sounds admirable, doesn't it? And it is: this is the longest period in European history that the major powers have not been at war with each other. On the other hand, being realistic, the glue that keeps Ireland in the EU is money.

The Brexit referendum was still a few years away at this point, but I couldn't stop thinking about it. If the UK actually left, would that mean that Ireland might also leave? Would Ireland follow its biggest trading partner out of this historic alliance?

And could Britain's exit lead to the breakup of the EU entirely?

Could Brexit lead to the end of peace in Europe? And, more importantly than all that, what about me? How would this affect me? How would it impact on my cultured, civilised and international life in the middle of Europe? And, even more crucially, how would this affect my chances of being able to drink quality local beer in Germany for the foreseeable future?

I mean, where else in the world would I be able to drink German beer at prices that are lower than water? Beer that doesn't give you a headache and that is available in bars that stay open all night? It had taken me most of my life to finally make it to the Promised Land and I wasn't going to be thrown out just when I was getting comfortable.

Then I came up with a solution whereby I could protect my German beer-drinking rights in this wonderful country: I could become a German citizen. Perfect, right?

Now, don't panic. I assure you it's not like Ireland was about to lose one of her favourite sons. My mother might not forgive me if I ever gave up my Irish citizenship. I wasn't even considering such a thing. But I'd found out something that would solve my dilemma and keep me in my mother's good graces.

It turned out that it's possible to have both a German and an Irish passport. But would I be able to meet the criteria required to become a German citizen? However much I loved the German way of life, would they accept me as one of their own? I had become so German in many ways, becoming more honest, working harder and sometimes even leaving the pub early.

But it's also true that, hard as I'd tried, I had not become fully German in every way. When it came to recycling, I still struggled with separating the green and brown glass. And I didn't have my own pair of house shoes.

More significantly, I still spoke bad German with a very strong Irish accent, and had made no progress when it came to German punctuality. Would I be able to fool the German system and get my German passport?

I started the citizenship process, and in a true test of my new German spirit of perseverance and resilience, this involved nearly two years of bureaucracy. There were endless rounds of paperwork, tests and interviews with even more endless questions about democracy and rights. Being from Ireland we know how democracy works much better than most other people. However, brown envelopes full of cash don't seem to be the way to go in Germany. I would just have to knuckle down and pass the tests.

Then there was the final interview. It was like the TV quiz show *Who Wants to be a Millionaire?* with all the stress and none of the money. But there was a German passport at stake. I was nervous, my pulse was racing and my adrenaline was high. But I was ready to try and pass as one of the locals. And for once, I was punctual.

The questions came in rapid fire and they were all in German. It was a blur. I'm not sure what the questions were and I'm even less sure what I said. One question I do remember, however, was that they asked me which terrorist organisations I belonged to. For the record, the answer is none ... unless you can count being baptised a Catholic. Finally, it was over and, after adopting an entirely non-readable expression a Buddhist monk would have been proud of, the interviewer suddenly smiled, 'Congratulations, *Herr* Kelly.'

I'd done it! After all the worry and stress, it was finally over. I had got my German passport; I was officially German. I was so proud – in a German sort of way; that is in a subtle and understated way. My future in the Promised Land was secure.

My next step was to go home as a dual citizen. But would I still be accepted back in Ireland?

CHAPTER 16

Going Home: Irish-German Soul

So how has living in Germany changed my life? First of all, when I go to the pub on a Friday night, I needn't be fashionably late. I am also able to leave before closing time with my head held high. I have important things to do on Saturday morning like a good German; things like cleaning my flat and sorting the rubbish for recycling.

Perhaps I am also more reliable and honest as a result of having lived among the Germans. I do like to think some of it has rubbed off on me. Okay, maybe I'm not as reliable as a BMW, but I'm certainly more honest than a Volkswagen.

When you live abroad in a non-English speaking environment, you have the chance to expand your horizons and learn a foreign language. And, yes, I have learned German, though not very well. (So now that's two languages I can't speak fluently.)

I've even started using Germanisms when I speak English, words like 'handy' and 'beamer'. No one back home would ever call a mobile phone a 'handy'. And in English-speaking countries a 'beamer' is slang for a certain German car that you drive, whereas in Germany a 'beamer' means a projector that you can use in the office. If you get these words mixed up, it can lead to some very interesting misunderstandings. Try telling some Germans that you drove your 'beamer' on the motorway and you won't have to wait long for their looks of puzzlement and confusion.

But it isn't only word choice. Spelling was never a strong point of mine, but my spelling in German is even worse, dramatically so. And as an additional present from the language gods, my English spelling has deteriorated further due to an overdependence on spell checkers with US settings. So now I spell like an American. What an embarrassment.

Another thing I've not been able to completely master is being on time. At the beginning, my problems with punctuality used to annoy my German friends. But when I meet them nowadays, they all arrive even later than I do; now it's always me waiting in the pub for them to arrive. Who could have predicted Germans becoming more relaxed about being late? Though they assure me it's an exception they make only for me.

And this might surprise you, but now that I'm officially half-German, I've also been thinking about changing my name. Mel Kelly sounds obviously Irish and I was thinking I should trade it in for a much more German-sounding name. I have received several suggestions, such as Michael Müller, Franz Schmidt and Jan-Ulrich Meyer.

But I'm not sure any of those suit me too well. Besides, I want to keep something of my Irish roots. So I was thinking of combining my original name with one of my German footballing heroes. How does Sami Khedira Kelly sound? Or maybe even Mel Jérôme Boateng? They both have a nice ring to them. Maybe one day.

I went back to Ireland a few weeks after getting my German citizenship. As I went through passport control, I produced both my Irish and German passports and excitedly asked the border guard which passport he wanted to see.

He returned my goofy smile with a scowl of contempt and barked at me to keep going. A few years ago his gruffness would have offended me. But having lived in Germany for so long, I've toughened up and can handle this sort of thing without giving it a second thought.

When my mother picked me up from the airport, she was a full three minutes late and I found myself involuntarily shaking my head in disappointment. This was my dear mother though, and I thought it better not to say anything.

When I greeted her, as one does in Germany, with a kiss on each cheek, she almost jumped with the shock. This level of physical contact in Ireland is, as I've mentioned, considered abnormal. And on our way home, I started to notice how disorganised the roads and signposts were. I was getting irritated and couldn't help but quietly mumble to myself, 'This really could have been planned a lot better.'

I was just getting comfortable in the silence of our drive home, when my mother observed, 'You've said nothing for the last twenty minutes. Are you not talking to me or something?' Twenty minutes of silence and I hadn't even noticed.

She looked back at the road: 'Is it true about this German passport thing?'

I waited a moment; this was sensitive territory. Then I replied in my new honest German fashion, 'Yes, it's true.'

She simply shrugged her shoulders, shook her head and gave me a look of disappointment and disdain, as only an Irish mother can. I felt like I could read her mind, 'Who is this person?'

When I came home in the early days of my exile, there was a great fuss made out of me for the duration of my stay. Over the years, however, this attention has been reduced to about an hour, which is enough time for a cup of tea and a sandwich.

But there was something different this time and I got the sense that my mother was concerned. I tried ignoring it, but the next morning I knew something was wrong when she offered to make me breakfast. This was a return to the old levels of attention and I wasn't sure why. Without asking what I wanted, she had prepared sausage and beer for me – for breakfast. I was in heaven.

I asked, 'Are you worried about me?'

She looked at me for a moment then said, 'I was before, but now I see how happy you are. And no matter what, you will always be my son … my *Irish* son.'

She was glad I was making a decent living in Germany, something that I'd failed to do in Ireland. And as she said herself, though I was born in Ireland, it turns out I was made in Germany.

ACKNOWLEDGEMENTS

I would like to thank everyone who contributed to the creation of this book.

To Jack Vincent, who was my mentor on the journey of this book. To Florian Mueck, who helped me believe it was possible. To my writing assistant Ken Macbeth Knowles, who helped me convert my stage comedy routines into a written book format. To my editor Anna Goodall, for her endless ideas and patience.

To my book cover and interior designer Barbara Schelling, to my artist Henning Janssen, for providing such humorous and entertaining illustrations, and to my copy editor Jarrod Shepherd.

To my many reviewers, who helped me with the selection of the content and tone of this book, including Sabrina Weiss, Catrin Wittman, Julie Happ, Cearbhall O' Siochain, Amy Hamilton and Armin Hierstetter.

On a personal note, thank you to my wonderful partner Drazenka, for her unwavering support for me on this journey.

ABOUT THE AUTHOR

Mel Kelly came from Ireland to Germany in 2003 for an IT consulting project, planning to stay just a few months. Many years later, he is still here.

When Mel was younger, he found public speaking completely terrifying – he suspects the reason is that he spent too much time in front of computers. In 2004, he decided to face down those paralyzing fears and joined Toastmasters.

After a few short years, he not only got over the anxiety, but also discovered the rollercoaster-like thrill of public speaking. So much so that Mel became an award-winning speaker at the European level in English and even German, albeit with a very strong Irish accent. It's a passion he put to good use as a speaker, trainer and master of ceremonies.

In 2014, Mel started doing stand-up comedy and founded Comedy Club Munich, which has become the largest English-German comedy club in the world. The main reason for this is that it's the only one. Comedy Club Munich runs regular comedy events with English and German-speaking comics from all over the world. Okay, the English-speaking comics are from all over the world, the German-speaking comics are from all over Germany.

Mel has has now done comedy events all over Europe and even did his first comedy tour in 2016 in German with a group of Irish musicians and comedians. He also did a comedy tour back in his hometown of Dublin and also performed at TEDxTUM, Munich.

You can follow Mel's blog at **melkellycomedy.com**

REVIEWS

"Mel Kelly has spent years studying the difference between Guinness and German beer and the cultures that produced them. Mel's style is wry, conversational and rarely sober. You will get to know and love the Germans, the Irish and even one of Ireland's most irrepressible, irreverent and irresistible exports, Mel Kelly."

— Bob Mohl, Speaker, Public Speaking Trainer, Author

"Mel hits the nail right on it's comedy head when it comes to comparing the Irish and German way of life. Concise and very comically amusing."

—Mark Nicholas, Comedian, Musician and Welshman in Germany since 1979 (Mark'n'Simon)

"An Irishman's jolly, jovial German jaunt. A very funny, eye-opening account of humorous personal insights into the unexpected customs of the Bavarian culture."

—Simon Elmore, from Dublin, Ireland, living in Germany since 1979. (the other 50% of the incredibly popular MusiComedy duo Mark'n'Simon)

A very amusing and insightful read about an expat's experiences while adjusting to life in Germany. The perfect book to take with you on a long train journey."

—Naomi Isaacs, Life Coach, Author, Jazz Singer

17230397R10076

Printed in Poland
by Amazon Fulfillment
Poland Sp. z o.o., Wrocław